Get This As a FREE Audiobook via Amazon's Audible.com

Visit: Bookskim.com/free

Introduction

Maximizing Your Business with Facebook

The term "Social Media Marketing" is becoming common. While a year ago it used to be SEO or Search Engine Optimized content, which is basically content with a few specific keywords, put in here and there, the trend nowadays is with various social networking sites like Facebook and Twitter to increase the profile of a website. The Internet is evolving quickly and something new concerning how you can improve your site's profile is coming up almost on a monthly basis.

Specifically, with Facebook there is a lot of information floating around the net about how essential it is for businesses to be on their website. Yet, many businesses have an innate fear of social networking as such because of their concerns with data security. This is the dilemma that most SMB or Small to Medium Businesses face, whether to be on Facebook or not.

This guide's purpose is to discuss in detail what exactly Facebook is and how using it can help any small business become bigger than imagined through social networking.

What is Facebook?

Facebook is a social networking site that was launched in February 2004, by January 2011, it had garnered over 600 million users. It is now considered the third largest web based company in the US after Google and Amazon and usually has more visitors every day than Google.

Even though Facebook my not be considered large when compared to the behemoths that are Google or Amazon, its growth rate has been so fast that people now feel that ignoring Facebook is at their own peril. Even a year ago, Facebook was considered as something for the younger generation – in fact when it was launched first by founder Mark Zuckerberg; it was a place where his classmates and then his college mates at Harvard could share information about themselves.

However, this has seen a radical change. While last year the under 25 age group made up 58% of the population in Facebook right now it is has come down to 40%. This is not so much because younger population is not using Facebook anymore; they still are at the same pace they used to, but because of the increase of other age groups in new registrations. A look at the registration statistics will show this. The those between the ages 35 to 55 has grown at an astounding 277% while the 55+ age group has shown a remarkable 195% increase in new registrations. This is definite proof that the "young" sheen has worn out of Facebook.

There are also other reasons for this, like Facebook's new initiatives to include businesses, with their social plug-ins and authenticating user logins. Although their analytics tool is not as sophisticated as Google's it offers much more in details including demographic information that is invaluable for most businesses.

It is not that everything is to the positive, there are negatives to using Facebook, and primary among this is the fear of data leakage in organizations. Yet, everything has its negatives, and it only remains to be seen if the positives are compelling enough to justify having a Facebook account.

This guide will be divided into three broad sections, the first would deal with why Facebook is important for most SMB's, the second will deal with how exactly they can use Facebook to their advantage, and the last will be the negatives to using Facebook.

Why Facebook is Important for Small Businesses

Increase Web Presence
This is the most basic reason for you to do anything online, because it increases your web presence. Any business has only one objective, and that is sales, be it a product or a service. The only way to do this is to make people aware that you are providing a particular product or service. Companies spend between 3% and 10% of their total sales just to do this. In corporate parlance, this is called marketing, when you advertise in different venues so that you let people know exactly what it is that you provide.

With so much of money at stake companies are always looking for ways in which they can get the same kind of exposure without spending as much money and the web is giving them that opportunity. More than 75% of the population in Western countries has broadband connections at home; more and more people are going online for their needs. Sales are slowly but surely moving towards online, and many manufacturers are already taking advantage of this.

Amazon is posting a 15% growth each year,

and their profits have skyrocketed in the past couple of years. In fact, even during the downturn, they were one of the few industries that posted growth. There are a number of benefits to buying online, primary among them being lower cost and this benefit is hard to match in retail sales.

Many organizations have taken notice of this growth and even though their online marketing budget is only around 14% of their overall marketing budget, it is a large increase from last year's 8%. Everyone realizes that the future is online, but there are still a number of organizations that are still wary. It has grown so fast that it has caught many companies by surprise.

With its enormous reach, especially in certain markets and demographics where traditional marketing does not have much impact, Facebook offers an inexpensive, yet quite effective way to put your company's face on the World Wide Web. Just having a website is not enough and everyone knows this. While there are alternatives to Facebook is dominating the social network sites and their 600 million users force you to consider the amount of people that you could possibly reach. With Facebook now surpassing Google in the number of people who visit them every day, this is becoming more compelling.

Increase Brand Image

This is a carry on from the previous point. The aim behind increasing web presence is to not only increase the brand awareness, but also increase brand image. While brand awareness or brand recall is easily achieved with advertising, increasing brand image is a little more difficult. Companies spend years developing a certain image for their brand, and any decision with regards to a new product is taken considering if it will fit the brand image or not.

Online this is not as difficult. Although the basics remain the same, it is much cheaper to develop a brand online than offline. For example, customer service online is usually restricted to email and responses to blog posts and questions in the forum. This is much easier to handle, and much cheaper in fact, than real time call centers where people answer your calls.

Of course, emails may not be able to fully replace human interaction, but it can reduce it by quite a big margin. In the same way advertising as well as promotion of a product is much cheaper online than it is in the real world.

Brand building is all about creating an image of the brand in the minds of the people, and one of the easiest ways to do this is to increase the interaction between the general population and the organization. While having a website is the bare minimum that an organization should do, there is not much interaction you can have with your customers through your website. Many sites have a "contact us" link and some even have a complaints page where you can log in and put in your complaints, but doing so in Facebook just increases the personal touch.

For example, while if you manufacture toasters and if a customer has a complaint with it, there is not much of a different between asking them to log into your website and post their complaint and asking them to do so on your Facebook page. The difference is that in Facebook they will be connected to you, so that as soon as a response is posted they will know about it instantly. While companies that do not have good customer service may not find this to be of much use, companies that spend on customer satisfaction will definitely find this useful. Imagine if you have a team that has a turn around time of less than four hours for every complaint, this is a good way to make your customers really feel that you care by giving them a resolution in under four hours. Even if you had as good a team, there is no point in it unless the customer realizes it, and Facebook ensures that your customers do.

Of course, you can integrate all the different facets into your customer service so that they receive and answer via email or even message to their phone that their issue has been resolved, but this calls for resources. In Facebook, everything is available. If a person connects to you on Facebook you do not have to worry about anything else other than resolving their issue, Facebook takes care of the rest. Not only this, but the customer's own personal network will also be aware of your response, especially if he clicks on a "thumbs up" sign signifying that he was happy with your service. This may take time to build, but it gives you more returns than any other CRM tool.

Having a website is all good and well, but just as you have different clothing for different purposes, you need different tools for different purposes. The advantage of Facebook is that it has an already existing infrastructure as well as over 600 million users, while at the same time being cheap to use, so you do not have to spend any resources in developing a tool for yourself.

Increase Customer Interaction
Once again, this dovetails into the previous topic in that Facebook, as an existing

networking tool gives you the option of using it to interact with your customers, at no cost to you. Simply having a corporate page on Facebook means that you will get people who are interested in you come and visit you. In addition, anyone who clicks on your fan button will have your logo on his or her profile. While this may not be a big plus with many SMB's initially, over time a fan base can be created. Added to this is the fact that you are linked to these contacts' contacts as well, which will help maximize your company's visibility.

Because Facebook is a place where people network it is a great place for you to bring out any news regarding your company. For example, if you are bringing out a new product, mentioning this on Facebook is a good idea as it will help generate interest in the product.

You can use Facebook as a means of providing discounts to your customers if they purchase a product or service using their Facebook login, they will get a discount on the product. A simple example is the release of video games. When the smash hit Call of Duty 6 was released into the market, it was an almost instant hit getting so many downloads that their servers started to hang. Most of this was because of their shrewd marketing through the social media. Interest was generated in the game by targeting a few fans and sending them unique invitations to the next in series.

Studying how exactly they did all this mostly using Internet based tools is a lesson on what can be accomplished online, with the minimum of expense. Another company that sells software for different purposes uses its Facebook fan base as a pre-launch testing team to get feedback about the application.

How exactly you interact with your customers is up to you, just remember that Facebook offers you an existing network that you can exploit. Depending on how innovative you make this interaction, you can get huge dividends from little outlay in terms of expense and time.

Lead Generation
This is one use of Facebook that many people do not make use of. Facebook has a lot of information about its users, and this information is made available to others depending on the privacy level that the users specify. Whenever they use their Facebook ID to log into your site, (if you install this facility of course), Facebook will make available to you as much information as the user has in his or her public profile.

This means that when it comes to savvy people who are aware of how Facebook works, you may well only get general information like email addresses. Email addresses are useful tool considering that the email address on Facebook will mostly be genuine. When it comes to users who are either not knowledgeable enough about the different privacy settings in Facebook or are just not bothered enough, you can get much more information from Facebook.

This can help you not only generate more leads for your ad campaign but also target it to specific niches based on the information that you get from Facebook. For example, if you are selling fitness equipment, you will probably be able to target your campaign to those people whose profile lists anything related to fitness as their hobbies. Not only is the campaign going to be much cheaper, it is also going to be much more effective, because you will never be able to target the audience in such a focused manner anywhere else.

As mentioned, the amount of information that is made available to you by Facebook depends on the users themselves, so there is always the chance that users will not make much information available to you. Yet, this method is still effective because you will get the basic information that you know is at least accurate and not outdated.

This facet of Facebook is even more useful when you consider the kind of business you deal in. If your business is local in nature, you can focus your search to a particular geographic area so that you know that any leads generated would be useful. This is much better than spending time on worldwide customers who are not going to benefit your business in any way.

Gain New Friends
This may not be a top reason, but it still has its uses. For example, if any user wishes to be friends with you and clicks on the friends tab in your company profile page, you can configure your account to accept friends by default. That way every person who becomes your friend is accepted as one by you. You are not only connected to them, but to their friends as well through their Facebook account.

This may take a little bit of time to net results, but as a long-term option to increase the profile of your organization it is a good idea. This is especially true if you have a dedicated person to maintain the profile of the company and put in any information about the company on a regular basis. They can also respond to queries or take note of any complaints. You are creating a certain loyalty in your network by working to take care of their issues so that the next time they want something they will come to you. They will recommend you to others and your network will be able to continue to expand.

Since you are an organization here, you can basically connect with everyone who wants to connect with you and over time, your network can only increase. With the pace at which the virtual world moves, many people are actually saying that they get their news from the social media long before they get it from the mainstream cable news channels. People are starting to rely on Facebook to get information that they need, rather than go through the news and then filter out what they do not need. If you like tennis, but are not interested in politics, you can keep abreast of what is happening in the tennis world while not having to sit through the political news to get to the sports.

This kind of targeting means that your network will be full of only people who are interested in you as they have the option of leaving your network at any time. This becomes useful when it comes to sales conversions, which is our next point.

Selling

The first thing that you should realize is that Facebook is a social network site. This means that you cannot actively canvass for sales the way you would elsewhere. Yet, simply because there is such a large network out there, there are things that you can do to increase your sales using your social network.

To bring back the example of the launch of Call of Duty, the producers of the game started their marketing months before the launch of their product. They sent out coded messages to people who were big in the gaming world. This included not only die-hard Call of Duty fans, but also critics. The code had to be cracked, and when you did that, it gave the URL to a new game that was supposed to come out soon.

There was nothing about Call of Duty in this strategy at all, yet because the URL had short scenes from the game, most people knew that it had to be Call of Duty because it coincided with their release schedule. This led to a storm of activity with gamers discussing about the merits and demerits of the new game, and all this without any basic information regarding the actual game.

When the activity levels started to die down a carefully choreographed leak would send the gamers into another storm until finally when the game was actually released there was so much demand for it that it grossed $410 million on the day of its launch, an all time record, putting to shame high grossing movies like Harry Potter.

Most of this was done only using social media, and even if Facebook did not play any part in this, it still shows the potential that an innovative strategy can have on sales. In addition, all this would not have cost 1/100th of the cost of traditional marketing. The producers were shrewd enough to use the strengths of such a network and the results are there for all to see.

Of course, the product itself was a good one, and the previous editions of the same game were top sellers themselves, so the producers had a base from which to work. The basic principles however do not change.

There are a number of other companies that use their Facebook fan base to do beta testing. The advantage of being a fan of the organization is that, you get to do free beta testing, and they get a discount when they do buy the product. This is a win-win situation for both the network as well as the company because their fan base will assure them of a minimum number of sales.

The kind of strategy depends on the kind of product you have to sell, and you cannot very well do beta testing for a new landscape design, if that is what your company does. Yet, it gives you the opportunity to try something really innovative, and the best part is that this is not expensive at all.

When Call of Duty had its beta testing, they had to rely on their fan base built over years but through their own network built at their own cost. Now, you have the opportunity to use an already existing network to try out your own unique marketing strategy and at little to no cost to you.

Community Pages
This is the reason why many manufacturers are wary of Facebook. Facebook launched their community pages in April 2010 and created a furor of complaints about how it was not only useless but was actually damaging for small business owners. Facebook has since gone out of its way to educate people on what exactly the community pages were and how it could be used.

The community pages is a feature that you can create in Facebook, much like a forum or a blog. It is easy to set up and you can have your own community. While this may not be absolutely necessary considering that

Facebook in itself a networking place, a separate community page gives many advantages.

When Facebook launched this initiative, it created a few hundred thousand community pages by default based on information they had about existing networks. Many businesses thought that this was not only pointless; it was an infringement because these pages were not created by them. These pages were, however, totally community driven, and while there were pages with as few as one or two fans, there were others with thousands.

While this left most businesses thinking that they had gotten the short end of the stick, over time these community pages actually started serving a useful purpose. Most of the more online perceptive companies employ a few people to search the net to gather information on what exactly is the public perception of the organization. While in the real world this is usually done using polls, it was much easier and cheaper to do so online. All one had to do was to monitor these community pages, or forums to know what was being said about the organization. If there were complaints, it did not take long to track these members down and mail them regarding their difficulty.

This was a huge opportunity for organizations

that were willing to take the bull by the horns. While these forums were community driven, it gave organizations an existing framework where they could deal with customer service issues. This strategy is simple, yet effective, and Google is a good example for how an organization can use these forums to their advantage.

When Google released their browser "Google Chrome" there were a number of issues with it. In fact, many critics said that it did not deserve the Google name. There were so many complaints about the browser that if you look back now, you would wonder how it survived the beta phase itself. Google tackled this in a unique way. They had a Google employee keep track of these forums and answer any complaints that came up. The effectiveness of this strategy can be discovered when you consider that the stable version of Chrome was launched in December 2008. By Jan 2011, it had garnered an 11% share in the browser market and was the third most widely used browser in the world, rapidly approaching Firefox's share of around 30%.

With the number of faults that the beta version had, this kind of growth is surprising. This is even more surprising considering that when the beta version was launched in Sep 2008 it hit 1% almost immediately. By

October, however, this had dropped to 0.69% because of the number of issues it had. Yet, they have reached 11% in just two years. Most of this is because Google kept its ear to the ground, had employees tracking forums where the faults were discussed. In many cases if a solution was not possible a bug report was filed in the customer's stead and the link was posted back to the forum. This generated a lot of goodwill so many users continued to use Chrome because they were sure that people were working to sort out the issues.

Although these community pages are just another kind of a forum, the advantage this gives is that it is within the Facebook network. This means that all users get the advantage of being connected all the time.

Use Facebook as an Advantage

There are a number of ways to do this. Being on Facebook is not an end in itself; it is only a means to an end. You should start looking at Facebook as a tool that you can use, and if you change your mind to think this way, you will start thinking of different and unique ways to use Facebook to your advantage.

For example, many top CRM tools can be quite expensive, but it is money that will have to be spent if you want to give your customers a good customer service experience. Yet,

Facebook offers you the advantage it being used much like a CRM tool but is totally free to use. It is also not as resource heavy in the sense that you do not need as much labor because of the way in which Facebook is designed.

While this is only an example, it shows how Facebook can be used in unique ways. There are several other ways in which Facebook can be used to maximize your business potential. Starting from the basic things that every SMB owner needs to do, we will discuss all these techniques in detail.

Create a Personal Profile

While your company needs to have a company page, it is imperative that you as the owner should have their own profile that you can link with the company. This is important because of the way Facebook users behave.

One of the most common behavior patterns of most Facebook users is to check out the profile page of all their friends, and those that they are interested in. While your company may have its own profile page on Facebook, most people are aware that the company is just as good as its management is and so will be interested in finding out about the owner.

Facebook operates on a platform of total

transparency and trust. This is why except for any portion of your profile that you purposefully keep hidden under different privacy settings, everything about you is open to public view. Most people do not have any problem with this, and most only make sure that they keep private information like home address, or telephone numbers hidden. If your company's is a stand alone page and does not link back to its owner, or top management, it sends out the wrong signals.

Facebook users want personal information. They would like to know if you are married; have kids, what your interests are, general information that however makes them feel that they understand you better, rather than just a one-liner saying that you are the owner/proprietor of a small business.

Not only that, but people that you link with on a personal level will be connected to your company as well, and those who come across your personal profile will be prompted to check out your company's home page too.

Even if this does not net you any business and there is no reason why this should not, it will at least increase the page views on your company's profile. Since Facebook is public, Google will rank your company's page based on how many clicks it gets internally on

Facebook, meaning that you have another way of increasing your company's exposure on the net.

Facebook News Feed
This is one of the most useful things about Facebook for most SMB owners. Facebook has two different kinds of news feeds, one is a mini feed that is free to use and another that is the main news feed. You need to pay to use the main news feed or be willing to build an application for it, but the mini feed is free and works just as well if used properly.

The mini feed is supposed to be a place where friends can find out what has happened with others in their network. When a Facebook user networks with you on any level, Facebook adds a mini feed to their profile that feeds back to you. When you publish anything, it is sent via this mini feed to your entire network, and if what you have to say is exciting, you can crawl across various networks getting exposure in the hundreds of thousands in a matter of days. All feeds from a user's network is amalgamated into one home page that is the first page that comes up when they log in.

The kind of exposure that this gives is enormous because most people are interested in knowing what is happening within their network. Of course, with Facebook's preoccupation with spammers, it would not be a good idea to use this feature as a marketing ploy. Even if it is not stopped now, you will actually be shooting your foot in two ways. You will be causing people to leave your network in droves because they find that all you have to say is promoting some product or the other. All they have to do is to unsubscribe to your feed, and you have effectively lost your network even if they remain connected to you through other channels. You will also be bringing yourself to the notice of Facebook administrators, and if they shut down your account for spamming, you have lost months and maybe years of hard work for nothing.

However, it is still a good venue to pass along information. For example, if you sell software, and want to do a pre-launch beta testing for a new iPhone app, sending out a feed that Facebook users can use their logins to download the app is a great idea. Not only will people in your immediate network connect to try out the software, this news is sure to spread across other networks giving you huge numbers. In fact, you will have reached millions of iPhone users within a matter of days, and every Facebook user who has an iPhone is a potential candidate. Many people actually use this beta testing for two purposes.

One, to get feedback about bugs in their

software, and second is that many out of these numbers who download the software to try it out do so to find out if it is useful to them. They are not doing it to give reviews, although there are a few who do that. Thus, if your software is good enough, most of these numbers will pay the conversion fee when you go online with it.

You may have to give a discount, but considering that you already have a specific number of users, you can afford to do this. Of course, if you do not give any discount, chances are that the next time you do any beta testing, the numbers will fall drastically.

This strategy will work for any sector you are in as long as the feed is designed in a unique way. The unfortunate thing is that you cannot afford to have deals like this often. Once or twice a year is about the maximum. Yet, it is deals like this that gives you the maximum exposure. Using a like strategy to bring your company to the notice of a large number of people is the idea.

This is the baseline of all marketing, and using Facebook to do this is not only inexpensive, it takes only a couple of minutes to set up. As long as you have taken precautions to ensure that the increased traffic does not cause your site to crash, setting up the feed should take less than 10 minutes.

Facebook Groups

Having your own groups section on Facebook has a number of advantages. You can have as many members as you like, and if people interested in what you have to say or are excited about your group in any way, your group can grow quickly.

Stephen Colbert's group went from zero to one million in just under nine days. This shows the power of having groups, and while you may not be able to get so many people excited about your organization, it is still a place where you can connect to your network and send out bits of information as many times during the day as you want.

Creating such a large group is not always easy, and unless you have something really compelling to say, you may not be able to create such a large network. This however does not preclude this option from the list of possibilities.

Facebook Pages

Facebook pages are a lot like Facebook Groups, but you get some extra advantages. This function was mostly created for small business owners who want to use Facebook to increase their company's profile on Facebook.

You get more screen space where you can include what you want, and you are able to customize it better using standard HTML or even flash. Although, some people feel that having a page on both Groups and Pages is not really necessary. Yet, this is another avenue, and you never know if one page will do better than another until you try and evaluate it.

Notes and Photos
Everyone knows that Facebook is primarily a place where you can share what is happening with your life through photos. Few people use Facebook without uploading photos into their profile. Starting from one on their profile page, and going up to creating different albums for different events, Facebook is much better than any other application because it offers the ability to upload unlimited photos.

There are many people who use Facebook as a place where they store their photos. It is online and therefore available at any time, and there is no way that you are going to lose your information because it is all maintained by Facebook.

When it comes to business, photos are an even more powerful medium than the written word. You can have pictures of events that you had in your company, like a Christmas party, a day out with all the employees, or other function you want to show.

You can even include pictures of your office building, but it is better to get everything with a casual setting than a professional one. The reason for this is that all said and done Facebook is a networking medium that you are using for your own business reasons. If you have only staid pictures, as is usually found on company brochures you will not get much mileage out of it.

The idea behind putting pictures in Facebook is to show what a fun place to work your organization is. It is to show how your whole company is like one big family, and while you earn money, you do not forget to enjoy life in the process. People appreciate the personal touch and more so in Facebook because they expect it.

Using the picture gallery as a place where you can upload photos of your products is really not a good idea. There are two reasons for this. The first is that it really does not say anything personal about you or your company apart from making you out to be a sort of person who is just using Facebook to market his products.

The second reason is that you can tag these photos. While photos of employees is not going to net you much gain because you will already be connected with them, there may be other photos with people outside your immediate network, like when you go to a business meeting or outside function. When you "tag" these photos, that person will be notified, prompting them to come visit you, and if you are lucky join your network. If he or she is a businessperson both of you will profit by being part of the other person's network.

This presupposes the notion that people you want to connect with are already in Facebook, but with Facebook showing the kind of rapid increase in new registrations that it is, they are either already there, or are planning to be.

Messages
Messages are a way for you to contact people who are outside your network. In other networking sites, generally you need to be connected before you can start sending and receiving messages, but Facebook offers you the alternative of actually sending messages to people who are totally outside your network.

This has a number of uses. For example, you can use it like an email to get in touch with people with whom you may other wise find it difficult to get in touch with. You can increase your network by getting in touch with people who have a large network of their own, but are totally unconnected to you to find out if you can connect with them. Just sending a friend request may not net you an answer, but if you message them directly, you may receive a positive response. You can even contact people and approach them directly about the service you are offering.

Facebook has done a lot of work to weed out spammers because this messaging facility was being used to send out spam messages. If you do so, Facebook will shut down your account, so you need to be careful about the number of messages that you send out to unconnected people from your account.

Yet, this is a powerful tool if you use it in the right manner. As long as you have a marketing strategy in place, you can find ways to use Facebook that will give you the same results, but with much lower costs.

Facebook Marketplace
The Facebook marketplace is a place where you can put up your advertisements. This is free, but if you overdo it, Facebook will once again penalize you because they have taken spammers seriously. Having your account shut down for spamming is not good for your company, especially if you have gone to a lot of trouble in building up your network.

The marketplace does not give you too much of a response, but if you are serious about something, coupling it with other applications that Facebook provides may give you a lot of dividends. The advantage of Facebook over other places like Craigslist is that everything ties into your Facebook account. Thus, if you want to hire more people, this may be a good option because people who come to you through your marketplace ad will already have checked out your company profile and will apply because they think that it is a good fit for them.

In the same way if you are offering a limited time offer on your products, although you will use other Facebook apps to let this information out, having it posted in the marketplace ensures that even people who are not connected with your network can come and take a look.

If your offer is good, it is sure to make its way into other networks, giving you that much more exposure for your business while at the same time, not having cost you anything to set up the entire campaign.

Paid Services

All the above techniques are ways to use Facebook's service for free and get the maximum exposure. Facebook also offers advertisers and others who are willing to spend a little money a lot more options and these are discussed next.

The amount of money you spend depends on the size of your target audience, and the length of your ad run. While short run ads can cost you only a few dollars, there are options for you to take advantage of sponsored ads that can cost in the hundreds of thousands.

Social Ads
This feature was brought out in 2007 by Facebook specifically for businesses because it allowed targeting of certain demographic groups within Facebook. You could target your ad based on age, sex, location, keywords, relationship, education, workplaces and basically any other field that you enter into Facebook.

This gives it a huge advantage over other tools that rely mostly on keywords. When you compare them to Facebook, you can see how narrowly you can target your audience. Not only this you can target your audience on other parameters like for paying for newsfeeds. These ads generally have a much higher return than sponsored ads.

Yet, another way is to target people who have approached you, or have browsed through your profile or your companies profile in the recent past. This gives the maximum click through ratio and is one of the best ways to get a response to your advertising.

On the other hand, sponsored ads are probably the best when it comes to brand building. Depending on the kind of marketing strategy you have, you can choose the kind of applications to use. While initially this kind of focused targeting may not have given many returns simply because the number of users were not too high, with over 600 million users and climbing, it makes good sense not only because you can configure your marketing strategy much better, but it is also good experience for the future when Facebook will play a much bigger role in advertising strategies.

If you are a large player, or have a marketing budget greater than $50,000, you can contact Facebook directly to configure your strategy even more. All you have to do is to contact them and tell them what you are looking for, and you will receive a call back from Facebook with various solutions to your problem.

Market Research

With Facebook offering the kind of specific information about its users that it does to advertisers, it is easy to focus market research within your target audience, and have results within hours, if not days. Polls are conducted all the time and many times frivolous questions will garner huge responses. This is because Facebook is looked upon as a place where you can be yourself, so the more natural sounding the questions are, the better the feedback.

Although, this may mean that getting through an entire market research campaign may take some time, it also means that the chances of you getting accurate useful information is even higher. While market research companies have not started using Facebook extensively because of the problem with getting users to answer a list of questions, as long as you plan it ahead of time and schedule one or two polls a day, you are sure to get a good response.

Facebook Platform

While this may not be of great use to all organizations those companies who are in the field of developing applications may find this useful. This is because Facebook promised all application developers that any application developed on the "Facebook Platform" would receive as much exposure as the app deserved, and that they could monetize these applications without any interference from Facebook.

This has given birth to a whole lot of companies that develop applications that you can use in Facebook. A simple example would be the "Family Tree" app that you can use to get in touch with family that you may not even know you had.

The quality of these apps may not always be consistent as they are not developed by Facebook but by third parties, but then it is the good ones that get the most use. If you are not into application development, you could still use these apps to advertise as you can focus your ads even more if you feel you need to. You can even approach organizations that develop these applications to sponsor them directly. Examples of this happening are "Drink sharing" apps developed with the sponsorship of beverage companies, and "Winking" apps developed with contact lens manufacturers.

There are other ways to use these applications. Companies that have large marketing budgets can create their own applications. These applications need to be installed into each user's profile by them, so the apps need to be good at what they are meant to do and also be eye catchy enough for users to want to use it.

This happens quite a bit in open source browsers. Both Mozilla's Firefox and Google's Chrome have the add-ons section. These applications are not created by Mozilla or Google, but by third party vendors. When you install these applications into your browser, you agree that these third party vendors can access a certain amount of information about you and your online habits. The apps on Facebook work pretty much the same way. Even if you are not collaborating with anyone to create these applications you can approach them for targeted marketing purposes.

Other Ways to Use Facebook

Until now, we have been discussing how companies can use Facebook directly for their purposes. Apart from these, there are other ways in which companies can use Facebook, and that is by linking their site with Facebook. There are a number of ways to do this, and each of them have a different purpose.

Social Plug-ins
If you have visited sites where you have seen a "Thumbs up" button, you know what this is.

This is the most common way to integrate your site with Facebook. This option may not sound like much to people who are not too "connected", but for those who are, it makes a big difference.

The reason is that simply by logging into Facebook and remaining logged in, all Facebook users can integrate their browsing experience into their Facebook profiles. If they have visited a site where you feel that you get great bargains, all that the user has to do is to click on the "I like" button. This will connect with their profile on Facebook and let their network also know where this "deal" could be found.

As a company that is offering this deal this has a huge impact. While you can expect a certain amount of traffic generated by word-of-mouth when your website a deal; it in no way compares to the exposure that your site will get if you include the Facebook Social Plug-in in your page. Just one Facebook user clicking on the button is sufficient to make this known instantly to his network. With the number of people who are online these days, the chances of you getting a number of Facebook users is high. This means that you can get much higher levels of activity in your site than if you did not include this button.

Authentication

This feature is when you use the Facebook login as yours. Many sites give you the option of creating an account with them, which will make your browsing experience that much better. This is not only for forums and blogs where you can actively follow someone, but also for sites that sell products.

Having a Facebook integrated login means that you are making their logging in into your site that much simpler for them. Just as in any other plug-in from Facebook, all you need to do is to copy a few lines of code into your site and you are good to go.

What this does is that you have a button offering users to log into your account using their Facebook account. When they click on that button, their log in or registration screen is pre-populated with their details. When they click on the register button, they will be prompted as to the amount of information that they wish to share with you. Even assuming that they wish to share only the basic of information, you are still ahead because you get more information about your users than you would get if they registered without Facebook.

What Facebook does is provides you information that is in the public domain about their users; even general information like age and sex matter a lot when you are analyzing your site's performance. Having more information simply means that you can focus your service that much better.

For example, if you are just an affiliate site who markets different products, there are a number of things that you have to keep in mind when choosing the kind of product to sell. Even after doing all this work you will still have to ensure that your site is responding in the way that you wish it to. For example, if you are selling washing machines, you would definitely appreciate knowing what percentage of your visitors were women, and what age group they fall under.

Even if it does not make you change your mind about the product, it will at least tell you what kind of content you have to focus on to pull in your target audience. When you are used to working only with keywords, having specific demographic information about your visiting public is something that nobody will say no to.

In fact, you can even personalize your user's experience by pulling in information from Facebook regarding to particular users. You can bring their news feeds into your site, so that they are still in touch with their network, and you can even use information about your users to individually tailor make user home pages to reflect their preferences. For example, if you know that your user is a 55+ aged person you can create a different "Welcome" page than if you know that your user was an under the age of 25.

In the real world, all businesses make use of information like this to make the customer's shopping experience better, and it is only a matter of time before it happens in the virtual world as well.

Facebook Negatives

With all these advantages, it is easy to think that using Facebook does not have any downsides. Just as in everything in the world Facebook has its downside. Some of them are little more than minor irritants, but others are big problems, big enough for large organizations to have kept away from Facebook.

Data Leakage
This is the biggest and probably the only problem when it comes to companies joining Facebook. Even if all the security in the world is made use of to protect data and make it

secure, there is nothing that can be done with the people working there.

Many employers feel that giving access to Facebook is dangerous because it is possible for company employees to share sensitive information with their network most of whom would not be employees of the same organization.

Some of the biggest problems to come up with Facebook are those that deal with employees ranting and raving about their organization on Facebook. Many employees have found that their comments about their job have even cost them their job. Yet, this is a small irritant when it is compared to other bigger problems.

For instance, there are a number of organizations that forbid the use of phones inside the office, and employees are not allowed to access their mail. However, they may be online and access the Internet because their work calls for this. A corporate firewall usually enforces this.

Although a corporate Facebook account can be useful to send messages to others within the same organization, and even share information, making their workplace a little fun too, it is dangerous because this network is connected to the outside world. If any employee discusses information that may not be restricted within the company, but is not meant for the general public, they may be putting their organization at risk. This is more so for publicly listed companies than for privately held ones.

From the point of view of employers there is no other way, yet, thinking back to progress, such restrictions have not managed to last long. It was not that long ago that the Internet was not given to employees, and before that, computers were thought of as a security risk. Now, even though phones are thought of as the same, most organizations do not have any problems with phones that do not have cameras. It is only when you have a camera phone that they have a problem.

Most of these restrictions have passed away, and so maybe in the future the restriction on Facebook will as well. It is therefore good to plan for that day because it will come. Many people thought that giving Internet connections to people would mean inside information going out. Now, most companies have realized that there is no such fear, and education employees on what can and cannot be disclosed to non employees has had better returns that restricting access to the Internet.

In fact, the only reason why companies even

restrict mail access is not so much that it is a security risk but that they feel that employees will spend too much time checking their personal mail rather than working.

Tone of Voice
This may sound a little odd, but a number of small businesses are finding it hard to modify their marketing to take advantage of Facebook. They have been accustomed to the traditional methods of advertising like newspapers, TV commercials and/or radio ads. When it comes to Facebook, the same formal voice that was used for so many years successfully just does not work.

Facebook prefers a more casual type of communication, and many users just ignore anything that even resembles formal communication. This means that all your researching and targeting of your audience will come to naught if you are not able to market the way the Facebook users prefer.

This is not a big hurdle, and is one that must be crossed. The Internet is the future, and sticking to "Tried and Tested" systems of marketing will not work in the years to come. Marketing in itself is dynamic and with the pace of progress online, it is even more dynamic. It is the person who stands out from the crowd who will be noticed.

With Facebook offering such a cheap way to advertise, many small businesses are taking advantage of this. This means that unless your advertisement is striking, it will be lost along with everything else, and not net you any benefit.

Transition Time

Facebook is evolving so fast that to them a couple of years is like eons. For most of us however, that is how long it takes for us to learn and get settled in something. For example, Facebook used their own take on HTML and called it FBML an acronym for Facebook Markup Language. Just when advertisers were beginning to get comfortable with FBML, Facebook dropped it in favor of iFrames.

As already mentioned, life online is really fast, and things happen in minutes. In the real world, life is a little slower. Most marketing managers are not necessarily tech savvy and it therefore takes them time to find out things and learn. They expect certain stability in their business relationship, and having things so dynamic that they will have to once again start from scratch and learn a new technology is putting them off.

Hackers

Although Facebook has taken hackers seriously, simply because there are so many users it is a little difficult to check each and every user. Many hackers use Facebook to gather a lot of personal information about people and companies that use Facebook. A number of high profile cases have come up in the past couple of years when hackers were able to put in their own code into a page and get even information that was blocked from public view. This has left a bad taste and there are a number of forums that are dedicated to anti Facebook people.

While this has no direct impact on a business as such it is still important because hackers can use your Facebook page to obtain information. This is an even bigger problem because Facebook will automatically find your page to be the culprit and block your page. If you are actively using Facebook in your marketing strategy you cannot afford to have your company page go down for a week while Facebook decides whether you were genuinely taken advantage of, or if you were deliberately doing something illegal.

One example of this was when a dating service put up pictures of topless models in their ads. Not only were their ads not delivered, their page was blocked. The company was not only a genuine one; it was a paid advertiser on

Facebook.

Although having topless pictures did infringe on the terms of use of Facebook, the company was of the opinion that they should have specified this in advance, or at least allowed them to carry on the ad campaign but with different pictures. Issues like these lead many to believe that Facebook has still not evolved to the stage when it can actually become a useful to businesses.

Conclusion

Going online is the future for all organizations big or small. Facebook is just one facet of this online presence. Marketing online is not limited to Facebook, nor can it even be considered to be the most effective. Yet, Facebook offers some compelling reasons for companies to use it to maximize their business.

There are both advantages as well as disadvantages to using Facebook, and it may well be true that it has still not reached the sophistication of other more established online names. However, with their popularity only increasing and showing no signs of diminishing, it would be rash not to include

Facebook into the overall marketing strategy.

At the pace at which Facebook has developed over the past few years, waiting until everything is set is not a good idea because at that time you will be totally unfamiliar with how Facebook works, let alone how to use it.

In addition, Facebook is not something that you use as a one time marketing strategy. It takes a long time, sometimes years to develop a network so unless you start now, you would not be able to take advantage of Facebook when you do want to.

In fact, this facet of Facebook, the time it takes you to set up a network, is one big reason for a number of marketing honchos to not think of Facebook. Even those who have actively started on Facebook find that the amount of time that they spend on Facebook building their network means that they have little time to even think of other social media.

It is important to remember that with all their imperfections, Facebook still offers a compelling reason for every business to be there. It is cheap and you can even do everything you want to for free if you want to. Although, you may not get the use of certain facilities that will definitely help you a lot, there are few other places where you can start off at free, and go up in stages depending on what your budget is.

It is effective – all said and done, marketing on Facebook is efficient. If handled properly just using Facebook for marketing is more than sufficient to get you the sales that you are looking for and once again if handled properly you do not even have to spend any money to do this.

At the rate at which certain groups grow, it all depends on you finding something of interest to which people can connect. If you do find that, there is every possibility that you too can have a network that measures in the tens of thousands. Once this network is set up, it is just following a few basic guidelines on what to do and what not to for you to immediately start seeing results.

It is the only way – however much some people want to deny it, Facebook as of now is the best choice when it comes to social marketing, and you do need social marketing. Even now everybody knows the value of door to door marketing and Facebook offers you the capacity to do the same thing but in a virtual environment.

www.ingramcontent.com/pod-product-compliance
Lightning Source LLC
Chambersburg PA
CBHW071243220526
45468CB00002B/976